AF482041

dedications

do i have to say it? you already know who you are & how the words go

there was no water

but i was still so scared of drowning.

i tied myself to the mast,
the raft, the high ground

i recorded elevation on my wrist,
cried and then panicked about crying

look, when the sea comes for us,
it comes fast. scrubs your skin raw

asks for your blood
& then your breath

and i just can't handle the salt, the sting,
the lakes gone sour from sidewalk runoff.

i went to the desert
& i still wanted to drown

but i wouldn't tell you,
just sat there and waited for rain.

I hope your dreams are amazing

I see you.
when you are hiding in the dim places,
mouth a stuttering skipping record,
shaking from cold/shame/fear/grief,
I see you.

I will put amethyst & kyanite
in every corner of your room,
spray salt water over all the entryways.
I have come with thread, gauze,
butterfly bandage.

Let the floods come, and, too, the drought.
The days of stony silence,
the long hours of sleep.

I have come with whispers, with shoulders
that will not give way beneath you.
I have come to watch you sew
your own heart back together.
I have come to hold your hand
as you pull the stitches through.

You push and I just pull you back to me
like we're dancing.

the boy is tired of being called naive

that boy takes everything too far,
stops breathing whenever he's
imagining hands on skin. calls
it time limit. calls it lung capacity.
the boy might be dreaming or
might be kissing in his sleep and
refuses to say which is worse.
everything he does is an attempt
to hide his face from the world
because his eyes are always crying
& his mouth is always laughing

& he's tired

the heart writes about the heart
after richard siken

& the things it might do if it was asked
the scent of patchouli, ginger lily, resin
rose quartz littering the bedroom floor
sweating off its skin and breathing hard
tracing all the stars outside the window
the heart writes about high saturation
a litany of frenzied metaphors in gold
sunlight, moonlight, ochre, willow branch
glitter and ink spilling over the black desk
teeth chewing lip & lip wanting soft touch
warm blankets fuzzy socks small lights
paint streaks chipped black nail polish
unnameable scent that lingers for days
clouds & weather, snowdrop, dew
the heart writes about another heart
and hopes that it writes back

the places i wanted to bite clean through

the palm of my hand
with its unforgivable itch
its too tight skin,
my own tongue scraping its
mismatched teeth, the line of my gums,
the skin between my first
and second knuckle
on my left pointer finger.
i wanted blood & viscera,
this song of teeth and jaw
overlying a pain that defied naming.
my inner wrist, where i can feel a pulse
undulating. i hated losing control as much
as I craved it, as much as i needed my life
to not be my life, my body to not be
my body. the soft, fleshy bits
of my upper arms. the curve
of all my major arteries.
i just wanted not to ache.

congrats friend, you're still here
for nate

one day, you're going to be the dust
circling a star ready to come undone:
all these bright things, bell laughs,
flash of fish in the rippling water unremembered
what would you be willing to leave behind
as the only proof of everything you've
        loved?
all you've touched & not-touched?
name yourself boy made tender from the
        fire
boy who has been through the autoclave
        and still
inhabits the spaces between where they said you could
not flourish
double sunrise, aching chest,
make a list of everything necessary to
        experience
in order to be alive the way you are alive:
the sound of petals unfurling.
google search "crucible meaning"
google search "rockrose"
google search "gently flowing bodies of
        water near me"
and god bless another year
where whatever has asked to kill you
has been told
no

*nate's own poetry can be found @ bloomingtrans (tumblr)
and poetrynate (instagram)*

instructions for an unspecified scenario

wake up!
burn the diaries
sweep the ash
kiss your knuckles
sweeten the blood

keep the promises
or come unkeeled
sit in the water
& find equilibrium

speak aloud
revolt against the silence
revolt against the stillness
eventually sleep

I called just to be quiet on the phone

came & kissed bruise from forehead,
brushed hair from eyes.
fate, forgive me my vices.
every lie i have told,
all the love I have failed to give
correctly. I have tried to find home
in everything. I have tried
to find home in everyone.
I daydream walking through a garden,
looking at beetles, talking about joy.
I want to love with my hands
& not my voice but the words
are so much easier to bear.

beautiful flares

whine like a dog when the fear hits
they will cut you open
                and it will change nothing
wake up with alchemy scars & maybe
        nowhere to sleep
spend the next fourteen weeks listing
what you cannot live without
you don't realize you're doing it

if they do not let you have this
        it may kill you
already the panic,   vodka and blood
please, promise me protection
from the fallout
let me rest where no one can see me
        tell me it's worth it
                tell me i won't break

no good reasons left

might as well scream but it won't do anything / my mouth
hurts from every kiss / i didn't want to regret them all but i
did anyways / you can't just grab people by the shoulders
and make them unhear your whimper / can't force them
to forget you ever gave ground / it won't pull the glitter
from their bedsheets / the back of his car / i threw up in
the wet grass and he took me home / you get over it and
then un-get-over-it / dear jude if you're reading this i'm so
fucking sorry / and for the dream i had where you choke
someone to death too / might as well be angry but my
teeth aren't sharp enough to draw blood / i don't want to
sleep in my bed / or someone else's / i don't want to sleep
/ i wish i was smarter with my mouth / i never will be
though

the boy isn't mad at you, he just can't feel anything he recognizes

you are friend & he loves you
he knows you don't want to hurt him
and right now that   is too much to bear
the boy trusts you. the boy is terrified.
the boy isn't sure
he deserves trust

look, speak softly to the boy
                              he cries
hug him. let him lean on you.
                              he cries
                              more
          he cries
          all the time

he doesn't want to be alone and he doesn't want to be
seen
like this
you are good. he believes you
when you say you love him
when you say it will be okay
but he's scared
and good things hurt
he won't always be like this

listen to the same song until you stop recognizing it

from where you are sitting, the fairy lights look like barbed
wire and everything's a noose. something is trying to kill
you. here is the routine: panic / scream / sob / stop it! stop
it! stop! / say something to make them all leave / dear god
but what
if they believe it / panic again / and why would you say it if
you didn't mean it / just to hurt them? / i can't breathe
there's something wrong / with my respiratory system
with / me
run scar gel over everything, from where you are sitting
it's fucking freezing and no one will get mad at you
the music stretches and loops and doesn't make sense
anymore, you can't remember what comes next & is it
even the same song no one will yell at you,
they're all quiet & concerned
you fucking hate it, you are possessed,
or is saying you're not yourself just an excuse
the evilest thing inside of you is still you, maybe
and it's not okay, it isn't fair, you can't keep acting like this
but how do you stop? what do you want?
when you get too tired to do anything
lie there this hollow thing of anger/terror/confusion
is that the end does it stop there (stop it! please!)
can you be coherent can you hear an apology
or forgiveness without splitting / open bursting
an organ crushing something in your fist
trying to forget you have blood and you have friends
and the sterile latex smell that reminds you of hospitals
try to sleep without counting (63-64-65-66-) don't sleep
the music makes your head hurt but the silence is terrible
can you be coherent can you be a person why the fuck
do you cry so much and for what and why are you angry

your dog looks at you
like she doesn't know what's happening
and you don't either and it keeps / happening

april 11th

if you let it this thing will swallow you
and if you don't it probably will anyways
i can't tell it no because i can't speak
and it wasn't really asking for permission
if it wants my body so bad it can have it
never did like it that much

the boy has been listening to that mallrat song again

someone kissed me once. it doesn't matter who. this is the oldest story, and the one i'm most ashamed of. someone kissed me once and all i knew to do was whatever i thought they wanted. i'd rather give in. i'd rather get it over with. someone put their tongue in my mouth and i forgot how to say no. i'd rather every bad thing be my fault. i don't know how to tell anyone all these things that i'm afraid of without sounding untrusting. someone let me cradle their face with my hands. i wrote the poems. all of them. i know how it sounds. if you write the thing as good sometimes it becomes good. not always. i don't have much room for regretting things. someone kissed me once. it was nice. i don't really think about what happened after that.

but i'll come back

teach me to stop / being ashamed
of my heart's
hysterics
                    so many things are
inside me
                                        unraveling
                and i keep peeling the skin from
        my lip
but pay it no mind. i promise / not to go anywhere
i can't return from
            everywhere else, though
                                    maybe

conversation with someone whose soul met mine like a strike-slip fault, with all relevant context removed

it felt like dry drowning

- *the fuse blows & suddenly darkness & quiet. for the first few seconds, it's peaceful, then the fear sets in*

I want to metaphor somewhere soft to sleep. not just for me

- *when your brain isn't working right you count to one hundred until it gives up*

does your heart curl like an adder? and you don't know why?

- *it splits like time lapse footage of a flower opening*

I tried to soothe it, bathe it in milk, pour honey & olive oil on its wounds, wrap it in cotton

- *it felt like dry drowning*

so many things do

- *the recurring themes. teeth, dancing*

I wanted to feel sad so I did and I wanted to cry so I didn't

- *I'm starting to forget which of us is which*

my mouth is dry and bleeding

-	sometimes I think poetry is the only thing I care
	about & sometimes I'd rather break my fingers and
	sew my mouth shut than make any more

*sometimes I get the urge to watch the sunrise but it usually
passes without incident*

interlude

i have not hugged anyone in three weeks. i have cried about this but i still don't text my best friend back. just say goodnight at 7:30 and put my phone on do not disturb. i lie in bed shaking, i whimper like a dog. from pain or pleasure. both make me want to curl up. like an isopod. or a pangolin. i think i know more about toads than voltaire did but i'm not going to elaborate on that. i can't stop daydreaming conversations where everyone says everything i'm afraid they're going to say. i don't really write in metaphor anymore, i just kind of say things that may or may not be true. also, i'm the sole force ensuring my friend maintains a stuffed animal collection into adulthood. i don't know if they know but when i fall asleep on them while we watch movies, that's a bigger confession of love than anything else i'm capable of. more than the poems too. lately i've been so scared to speak. and i don't really know what i'm making here. that's fine.

**the first step is naming the problem / but what comes
next**

whatever's wrong with you
never announced its presence

it just showed up and put sour
where other things should be
took your mouth and fed it carrion.

now you can't think right

well, nothing means much of anything to you anymore
                    but it holds you so close it's almost
                    like not being alone

second to last monday of the month

nothing to write today

it will come back

re-skin the deer,
string back together the bones,
braid muscle again to nerve &
return blood to capillary.
cycle back through every sunrise,
let each flower bud and bloom once more.
seeds sown over and over.
bathe in glow either neon or soft
(you pick)
un-cry. un-shake. un-hurt.
put that back where you found it,
it's not yours and you've no use for it.
all the light that has ever touched you
rises up and reaches out at the same time.
every ocean spills over
& brings us back to the devonian era
to give us a new chance for evolution.
find the person who first had the idea
to hold someone else's hand & hug them.
all flashing silver is just glitter-glint and fish
          scale.
pause for breath.

excuses for not texting back and also things i convince myself someone will say

sorry i was working / sorry i was sleeping / was taking my dog for a walk / can you stop being annoying? / and so clingy? / i was feeding my frogs / you say you love me so often it feels like you're trying to convince someone / cleaning the mouse cage / cleaning my room / i was burning something / not myself / actually it's better when you're not texting back / phone died / i was in the shower / i was putting on eyeliner / you're cold / you're performative / i don't love you / i wanted to hurt you / i was sleeping at work / i was crying in the backroom / your panic is high maintenance and probably not even real / i was picking up my prescription / i was writing / i just didn't see your text

**the poem that the therapist for trans people that i saw
one time and hated probably wanted me to write**

i don't recognize anything about myself
from before i came out, which is to say
17 years of my life don't belong to me.
i feel like i should wear that hat that says
    i'm sorry women.
i feel like i'm rejecting a gift
someone gave me.
i mean is it really that bad to just be a woman?
why can't i just be a woman?
      why do i have to make things hard?
my parents probably think this was a phase
because i've stopped correcting them
but if i got angry every time i was misgendered
i'd never stop being angry. so i let it go.
you know the thought of not
getting top surgery makes me want to die
      but i keep almost calling to cancel it.
i don't know why.
i can tell when people are just humoring me
& i'm sick of being pathologized and pitied.
it's not up to me though

love letter to my heart

the ancient greeks described eros as lack
and i don't want to love like that

oh, be full my heart
hold the sun inside of yourself
this warmth that does not swallow you
but takes you to the open spaces

oh my heart, my reckless heart
full of thistles and cattails and sky
do not make yourself a hollow of
wanting, a home of absence

be a wild thing, be constellation
be freedom, bright eyes, do not falter
do not wait for any other thing

oh, my heart, let everything
you seek be within you.

you say this like it's easy

if they're a knife be a sharper knife
        if they want to burn you, bring the floods
            the downpour. the deluge.
            the overflow and the
                    inundation
if they scream, scream louder
if they chase you, stand and fight
buy curved needles and practice suturing techniques
when they look at you
        in the way you do not want to be looked at,
        bite them
drag your nails down their forearm
leave a permanent scar
if they're cold be colder or be a heatwave
but don't ever let them win
stop pressing your palms to your face
stop asking for someone to save you
eat poison till you grow immune
if you have to

untitled 3/9/2020

i write in metaphor without saying it's metaphor. dancing. the feeling of the palm of someone else's hand. i recede and you follow. i'm not receding, i'm leading, and you follow. the music cuts in and out, the rhyme scheme falls apart towards the end, and you follow. i don't really like dancing but i like the pushing & pulling, leading & following- gentle and quiet and then i sleep.

notes

i hope your dreams are amazing was originally posted on my blog november 2019

the heart writes about the heart was originally posted on my blog december 2019. it was inspired by the line "Sometimes, at night, in bed, before I fall asleep, I think about a poem I might write, someday, about my heart, says the heart." from *the language of the birds* by Richard Siken

the places i wanted to bite clean through was originally from a scrapped project of mine called dentition from late 2018 / early 2019

congrats friend, you're still here was originally posted under a slightly different title on my blog october 2019

the title *beautiful flares* comes from a misread Teen Suicide lyric. the actual line goes "you know the flares they fire from sinking ships? / I haven't felt like this in a while". the poem was posted on my blog may 2020

in *listen to the same song until you stop recognizing it*, the song in question is *island garden song* by the Mountain Goats

in *the boy has been listening to that mallrat song again*, the song in question is *charlie* by mallrat

a version of *conversation with someone whose soul met mine like a strike-slip fault, with all relevant context removed* was posted on my blog december 2019 in *the first step is naming the problem / but what comes next*, the line "took your mouth and fed it carrion. / now you can't think right" is a reference to the line "i ate rich raw carrion till i couldn't think right" from *golden jackal song* by the Mountain Goats

a version of *it will come back* was posted on my blog december 2019

love letter to my heart was originally posted on my blog may 2019. i wrote it at inpatient after several readings of *eros the bittersweet* by anne carson

about the author

aster laurel montor is a trans poet from the midwest who takes too many photos of his frogs and mice. he can usually be found sleeping through movies or getting glitter everywhere. more of his poetry can be found on his blog, aphelionbruise.tumblr.com.